In a Boneyard in Galway

In a Boneyard in Galway

Poems by

Lee A. Jacobus

Hammonasset House Books
Clinton, Connecticut

Copyright © 2024 by Lee A. Jacobus

Except for short selections reprinted for purposes of
book review, all reproduction rights are reserved.
Requests for permission to replicate should
Be addressed to the publisher

First edition 2024

Printed and bound by Ingram Content Group

Book design by Lee A. Jacobus

Cover and interior photographs by Lee A. Jacobus

Hammonasset House Books
860.664.8028
www.hammonassethouse.com
1 Laconia Dr. Clinton, CT 06413

For Joanna

Acknowledgements

These poems were written over a period of time, in Ireland, in Boeing jets over the Atlantic, and at home. They owe a great deal to the enthusiasm of my students in the Modern Irish Literature class I taught for more than twenty-five years at the University of Connecticut. They also owe a great deal to my colleagues and other professors, poets, artists, and writers whose friendship and association over decades stimulated me and my love for the great literature of this tiny island. The title poem was published by Pedestal Magazine in 2024.

TABLE OF CONTENTS

In a Boneyard in Galway /11
Behind a Dublin Door /14
Ben Bulben /15
All of Ireland v All of England /16
86 St. Stephen's Green /18
At Queens University /19
Cararoe Is Upside Down /21
Connemara Teeth /23
A Cemetery in Wicklow /24
Young Ireland /27
Down in St. Michan's /30
O'Connell Bridge in June /31
Heroin at Mulligan's /33
Neary's Pub /34
In the Dandelion Market /35
Donegall Square /37
Belfast Pillbox /39
Gas and Tears /40
Saracen /42
Berry Street Now /43
Francis Stuart in Barney Kiernan's /45
The Book of Kells /47

After Hours at Patti Groome's /48
St. Stephens Green /49
Lift Your Pint /51
Sunday in Athlone /52
Wolfe Tone Fractured /53
Seamus Took My Hand /55
Time Out /57
Meeting Mary Lavin /60
Sheila the Maid in the Kitchen /61
All Too Irish /62
In the Shebeen /63
In the Muniment Room /64
Antrim /66
Patrick Kavanagh /67
Lucia Joyce /69
Seán O'Casey /70
Coole Park /72
The Taín Bo Cuailnge /74
James Joyce /75

In a Boneyard in Galway

In a boneyard in Galway
I stepped into an open grave
the grass above my head,
invisible, a vacancy waiting
for me.
        It was my fall from grace,
a shock as I penetrated the
darkness.
        I never felt so Irish
as at that moment looking up
at the cloudless sky,
a pallid window.

I scrambled
up the crumbling sides
though I was its only tenant.

Elsewhere the stones canted
with bleak messages. Culann age 6,
Aoife 44, Emer 63, never forgotten,
always remembered, but completely abandoned.

Plastic weathered toys
stood in for griefs that once bit
like January winds from the sea.

In the nearby ruin of a stone chapel
rainwater stood in the stoup. A blessing

in waiting.
        Within, a flowered brassiere lay
draped in the grass, girlish, cheerful,
tossed off like the hatch of an egg.

I placed it in the beautifully dressed
arched window looking out toward the sea,
hanging there, a flag for the living.

Johnny Finnerty's headstone
Died 1970 age 6
Cararoe, Ireland

Behind a Dublin Door

On the Wellington Road
behind a Dublin door,
the canon who Irished
Genesis sat with nutbread
and tea, while a granddaughter
crammed above.
                    He snatched me
from the sisters' bookshop
for my theology, talking
of Pareus and Melancthon
as if they were current
champions of the Church
of Ireland.
          An old man,
He recovered his youth
with eyes alive, his hand
pressing mine with
courtesies and cheer.
                    His
ideas endowed the upholstery,
the garnet-colored drapes,
and the dust in the carpets.

Ben Bulben

As I stood there and looked out
I saw no sign of Finn or the Fianna,
nor of ancient Irish heroism.

I turned my attention to puzzle out
the cryptic message on Yeats' grave,
his imploring the horseman to move on.

Perhaps a suggestion rather than
command, a hint to a traveler, telling him
to ignore the signs of death and move.

Life is not a symbol, it is not a time of rest,
but a time of action. Yeats is said to rest,
because he is stretched out below, the

way Ben Bulben is stretched out beyond.
In both action is implied, in a strange way
preserved, as if the future might release it again.

The potential of myth, the allure of Medh, all
point to a resurrection of sorts, but the grave stone
for Medh is a cairn whose circle is a navel

into the mysteries of Sligo and the past. It is rich
and glorious, but glory itself is a myth, and the
trick is to mount your steed and move on.

All of Ireland v All of England

On our way to Landsdowne
we took a route near the stables
and on the walk we saw
the flattened body of a giant
rat.
    It must have been, I thought,
the thrust of an excited mare,
or a feisty stallion putting up
with no nonsense on his way
to the challenges of the Nations Cup
jumping the bars with clean air
below because only a hero could
have mashed this rat with such
authority, such absoluteness
and mighty conquest.
                        Naturally
I thought of this as a sign. What
could be more oracular.
                        But then,
I also thought how Irish it was
to leave the leavings so casually
for us to see. Did no one clean up
after themselves?
                        Or was it an emblem
of something the English footballers
would recognize and factor into their play?

Landsdowne is gone now, but in 1973

we were tense with anticipation
when we took our places in the stands
and saw the early ruggers massing
on both sides.   It was a regularly scheduled
match in the Five Nations Championship,
a fiery football stew with Wales, Scotland,
England, France, and Ireland.
                              Would there be
trouble, we asked. These were difficult times
and exuberant fans on both sides.
                              But what
struck us was not the absence of trouble,
but the presence of honest emotion, almost
a spiritual expression in *Amhrán na bhFiann*,
The Soldier's Song, the Irish national
anthem, before the game, sung magnificently
with what we now call soul.
                              And, true, Ireland won
18 to 9. We exited the stadium richer
emotionally not because of a game won,
but because of a nation won.

86 St. Stephen's Green

It gives me pause,
Joyce sat here and listened
wryly, keeping track of every sound.
upstairs the prefect's fireplace
and echo of tundishes.
                        (The cabby
corrected us to "funnel"
as we drove through Drumcondra.)

In the Aula Maxima, the barn, a room
higher than wider
and longer than liver
he sat there too.
                        These are dead thoughts.
Men have come and gone
and the land wears thin over them.

At Queens University

Professors all, we met for coffee.
Joseph, a former Jesuit now engaged
with schools and travel, sat happily
beside Jonathan, a former Benedictine
married to a Jew.

Only minutes earlier we
paused at the bronze Winged Victory,
raising her wreath over a fallen
youth holding a sword.
                        The emblem
of Georgian morality in the posture
of Goddess and boy stands before
the fortress-like Lanyan Building,
whose windows belong
in a cathedral.
                  Here architecture
expresses church and strength,
the power of character and zeal,
while the realities of war
present themselves in myth
and sentiment.
                  Joseph the Jesuit
explained.
                  Remembering the dead was only one
of the functions of the university.

Jonathan the Benedictine puzzled us,
saying such memorials belonged
in city squares and cemeteries.

As we drank our coffee, we mused
over the alignment of the church and school,
the preparation and the sacrifice of youth
to the myths of heroism and nobility.

And, of course, we all three reflected on
our commitment to life and teaching,
while having, in our own different ways,
turned our back on sentimentalism and the Church.

Cararoe Is Upside Down

Carraroe is upside down
her feet are full of clay.
Grass has wings for stubborn doubt
and crosses iron our troubles out.

Houses sing on hills
and towers settle down
while waters lap
men's souls underground.

God knows the ground
is earthy there
where stones
have given way

and old men sing
their dry heart's tale
near peatricks
stacked beside the trail.

Cararoe is upside down
with water waking land.
Turf is all the stepping stone
and wild iris there alone.

Cararoe
Rocks, Gorse, and Soul

Connemara Teeth

Behind the bar in darkness
Maureen Flaherty stands tall and straight,
her frank eyes welcoming.
Her nervous mother wonders who of us
would do her harm.
                            Maureen
in the darkness, with the Irish
soft on her lips. In this dark pub
she glistens like emeralds and smiles
at the men with her beautiful teeth.
                            But the men,
their mouths full of brown age
and sour grief
suck the joy from the air.
                            Maureen,
dark Galway girl, hovers
for a moment in time.

A Cemetery in Wicklow

Like sex. I had to figure it out on my own.
We kept our Irishness hidden like a gold coin
in a black reticule. My Protestant name implied
security and confounded Father McDonough.

So, one June day with the sun warm
over my shoulder, on my way to Dalkey
the bus stopped for a glimpse of a tower
near the cemetery in Glendalough.

Struck by the Irish cross like the one in
Glassnevin, I suddenly found a parcel
of names I recognized as my forbears.
The signs on the canted stones spoke to me.

All the names of my cousins were there.
Martin Byrne, Edward Byrne, Julia Byrne,
Margaret Byrne, William Byrne, Robert Byrne,
with dates stretching to centuries earlier.

The English could not civilize the Byrnes.
They took flight but never surrendered.
Now, I understand the heritage of violence,
audacity, scrupulousness, and rage

that lurks deep in my blood, held back only by

my name, only by the mellowing measure of Dutch stubbornness, and my family's refusal to reveal their dark secret.

Family names in Wicklow

Young Ireland

Smith O'Brien rules the intersection
of O'Connell Street and history
while I stared up at him
worried that starlings may
shit on his wavy locks.
                      I was taken
with his poise, his crossed arms,
holding a scroll like a Roman
poet, but looking out away from England,
to the West country and freedom.

In 1848 O'Brien led Young Ireland,
another Irish rising that brought
him to the gibbet.
                  But a gentleman,
son of a baron, he escaped
with transportation.
                  A Protestant,
speaking Irish, demanding independence
and freedom for Catholics,
he chose exile to death
and now stands within feet of
The Liberator, Daniel O'Connell.

Within, a string of ironies,
strictly Irish.

                The strangest
was my son's outburst when he
saw the statue.
                "It's you," he said,
"Look. It's you." And I looked
at an image of my younger face
in stone. Were my Irish genes
echoing over the centuries?
Were they calling me home
after all those years of exile?
Was Smith O'Brien a siren
there on O'Connell Street?

William Smith O'Brien
Young Ireland, 1848

Down in St. Michan's

Above, Handel's memory is preserved
on the floor by his broken keyboard.
Only memory preserves Charles Parnell,
carried in and carried out, while
the Catholic crowds refused to
step into a Protestant church.
Huge iron doors lead down
to the vaults. Arched and mortared,
a thousand years old, the crypt,
where no flesh corrupts, holds
the Crusader, thighs broken and
crossed, with a leather chest
that flaps like a valise. His mouth
holds a hollow, thoughtful expression.
His dark shiny hands, like James I,
who never washed, lie beside
the Nun, his timeless bride. She
stares upward from her grave,
her head huge, her sex melted.

Nearby, vandals broke through
the evil Lord Leitrim's
century-old lead coffin,
but fled when they touched
his soft, fleshy hands. The living
flesh of Irish memory hides
here in generations of pain.

O'Connell Bridge in June

It was like another world,
my first day in Dublin,
down on the bus from
the rectitude of Ballsbridge,
only to be swarmed by women
wearing blousy flowered dresses
and bangles on their arms,
their hair free and touseled
with their little ones suddenly
alert and ranging about my
hands. No one warned me
about the gypsies, who
surrounded me with a sharp
sense that I was an easy
mark, and they were right.

Their cries made a familiar
music. I reached in my pocket
for a coin, clearly much
too grand for this occasion
because their reaction was
astonishment, the nearest
spirit took it from me,
and raising it high above her
head, she danced barefoot,
singing now like a diva,

inspiring away all the crew,
leaving me amazed and alone.
Industry, literature, and art
stood still for a moment
in the startling June sunlight
bursting from the Liffey below.

Heroin at Mulligan's

    Back in the pub a stir
Shows the girl, her eyes gone dead
Like bulbs in the morning, listing.
                                  The fellow
In the new suit was holding her up.
                                  Ryan
Comforted her–said a few words.
                                  But she fell
Across the Chairs
While the room grew hot and drinkers
Shuffled their pints about.
                              A beautiful girl,
Ryan said, between bouts. Tracks up both
Arms like a new-minted graveyard. Heroin,
Says Ryan, just on television news,

A celebrity. In three months time she'll be bones.

Neary's Pub

Moya, the Dutch girl
with sleepy, tolerant
Egyptian Eyes, supped wine
and gin. She had words only
for her girlfriend Claire.
                              Patrick,
gold ring in his ear,
dark hair long, and Emmet,
his red beard as Irish as dawn,
hoisted pints and talked of wisdom.
They thought to cheer the three
girls down the bar. "They're only
with their ma."
                         But Emmet called
for another pint and sagely said,
"Girls talk to girls in Neary's."

In the Dandelion Market

Down in the Dandelion Market
Stalls sprout
And beads spill
                          Beware of pickpockets
                          In the Dandelion Market

Early morning brings
Chancy fellows with their girls
For a day of hawking wares
                          Oh it's damp and it's cold
                          In the Dandelion Market

Motors and coils
And dresses and shirts
And candles and crafts
                          And everything's fun
                          In the Dandelion Market

The eyes of the hawkers
Nervous and sly
With merchandise over the counters
                          Everything's for sale
                          In the Dandelion Market

Down from the North
Come the pots and the pans
And the suits and ties
                          They even things out
                          In the Dandelion Market

Try these on, they'll fit sure
Lots of wear left yet
In these tweeds, sweet

                    See the hawkers smile at the sale
                    In the Dandelion Market

Bombs and broken windows
Left behind, but TV sets
Sell for a song, dear

                    Look it up, all's for sale for a song
                    In the Dandelion Market

Donegall Square

For me the statue of
Queen Victoria was
a curiosity, a typical
reminder of the past.

But to the few souls
I saw on the road
below, it had meaning
beyond pain and memory.

The chain link fence
I saw, driving slowly
in front of City Hall,
was fifteen feet high.

The point, they said,
was to make it harder
for a bomb thrower
to clear it entirely.

At that time bomb
throwers had good
arms, but the City
played hard ball

on defense. We had
already been through

The defenestration of
Hotel Europa, so

it was painfully clear
that defense went only
so far. We were advised to
turn our backs on no one.

Belfast Pillbox

Like medicine for a troubled
stomach, or a nightime *mal
de tête*, the pillbox I saw was
upstanding, rigid, firm, the
cure for any sudden attack
that might upset a patient
waiting inside the bricks
piled like aspirin tablets
cemented by urban mucus,
implacable. Hardly tall
enough for me to stand in,
only a three and a half foot
rectangle, placed brazenly
on the corner of Donegall
Place and Victoria Square,
like a masonry telephone
booth ready to send a
message abroad or within.

The snub-nosed gun looked
out on the statue of Queen
Victoria, prepared to swivel
through its eye-level slit to
challenge the gunman, or
the bomber, or political
infidel with a rebellious
slogan written in fire.

Gas and Tears

During the Troubles
I walked on the Shankhill Road
with a man who pointed
to the other side and said,
"He's a Prod," about a young
fellow who looked to me
to be about as normal as I,
and asked how could you tell.
"Ah, it's easy, you just see it,"
he said.
         And later that night the
area was cordoned and the
gas plops sounded in the streets
and many ran down with their
eyes in tears, while others ran
forward with stones in their hand
to reward the British with their skill.
Some roamed behind doors
with gas masks on, looking like
monsters from the Planet of the Apes,
goggle eyed, dog-ferocious,
and limping like wounded souls.

Mask and Canister

Saracen

We were walking up from the train
Station after having a coffee
in the hotel.
              We began to spread out,
holding maps like besotted tourists.
But I needed no map. I aimed my
camera right and left, excited at
being in Belfast during a rare truce.

Then, to my left, looking through my
viewfinder, I saw not only the
armored Saracen moving slowly
away from me, but then the back door
opening very slightly, almost delicately,
as if a costumed presenter was about
to make an appearance–but what I saw
was a Sten-gun pointed directly at me.

I lowered my camera slowly praying not
to alarm the young British soldier, whose
own anxiety may have equaled mine. The
point was to save my life, to avoid mis-
understandings. Threaten no one with
my camera, make no mistakes.
                              The North
was not my country.

Berry Street Now

Thirty years later, the headquarters
at Berry Street, Belfast, is now an
upscale shopping center, with a
vastness that took my breath away.

When I was there during the Troubles,
the entrance was sandbagged as if
expecting heavy artillery or maybe
a battalion of Mills Bombs or

Molotov cocktails. To enter, I went
down five steps into a dark large
room with a desk to the right. The
ceiling over my head was low

enough to make me stoop. The
commander in charge was dressed
smartly in a camouflage tight-weave
jumper because it was January.

I did not arrive there alone. I was
escorted by two large infantrymen
who had come up beside me on
the street without my awareness

and quietly took me away without
a word, leaving Joanna behind having
no idea why or where I was going.

I was being detained as suspicious.

The commander was polite, even
a bit raffish, as if we were in a film,
yet he quizzed me efficiently and listened
to my business: taking pictures, an

innocent occupation. Once he understood,
he agreed that I could continue, but as I
looked around, seeing a soldier playing
billiards, I asked to photograph right there.

My Lord, no, he told me. Anywhere
outside, of course. No installations, no
military configurations, nothing that
would invite inspection and danger.

Things were so polite, so efficient, so
upfront and explicit that I could not
but be grateful that there was no hint
of bloodshed, coercion, or hunger

strikes. Nothing like the front pages
of the newspapers, and nothing like
the terror on the Falls Road or explosions
in the hotels. And now, looking back

after these years of pain and murder
it seemed almost a paltry victory to
stand and look at the wide expanse
of Castle Court Shopping Center
where British headquarters once stood.

Francis Stuart in Barney Kiernan's

Yeats called him a dunce
and today he is named among
the chosen of Irish letters.

What I knew about him were
his years in Berlin when the war
fueled Ireland's rage
against England.
                    No Nazi,
but willing to puppet their
news, he managed somehow
to return in a halo of glory
and make home his town.

To be sure, I knew about Iseult
Gonne, the tragic beauty, whose
clothes he burned, whose face
he slapped, whose life he wrecked.

And now he sat across from me,
holding forth like a drunken lord,
whiskey in his hand, a grimace
on his face, enchanting the roomful
of his admirers, themselves drunk
on his glamor, and drunk on legend.

Lighting up the premises,
he leaned forward with a grunt
when I asked him what it was like

to be married to Iseult Gonne, "Damned near killed me!" he roared in a phlegmy country cough, as if he were putting end to a bad dream.

The Book of Kells

The slightness of it shocked me.
Kells was pale and wan like wheat in the dusk.
Blue uniforms, old men, hands behind back
shuffling the curtains and vaults of books
and busts of men dead to all those for whom
this shrine is not a postcard home.

St. Anthony looked back at me from the
goldsoaked page in temptation. Something
I had noticed when I stared at those pages.
Strange, not to notice earlier, as if temptation
were no thing I knew or feared.

After the Shelburne and the Byrnes'
and the walk in the rainy dark
down to the Liffey, with Gardái
ringing their ways in the distance,
we pressed a florin to the glass
and were ushered into the darkness
of Patti Groome's where politicians
drink and the talk is mumbled intimacy.

Dermot, the predatory solicitor,
drove us home but did not separate us.
St. Anthony walked with me back to
Herbert Park in a sacramental drizzle,
aware that temptation had many forms,
and of none of them was I immune.

After Hours at Patti Groome's

In those days when after hours meant
illegal except in select hotels for bona fides,
we raked a coin across the windowed door
where we stood hearing soft bellowings
behind the curtains and in the silky dark
until the door whisked us into
society.
        We were led to a table amid the
crowd. The voices around us seemed noble
in their way, not loud, not crackling with
anger or smudged by sentimentality. No,
these men, and they were mostly men,
were not conducting business, or seemed
not to, despite their intensity, their blurred
vocality.
        The legend was this was a barracks
for the Fianna Fáil in mufti, off duty, in the
town for a night of ease.
                At the right moment
Patti herself came down the stairs like an
older Barbara Stanwyck, taking notice of
all the regulars, smiling at us nobodies, sipping
at our stout.
        It was a performance. The entire
evening was a performance.

St. Stephens Green

Her statue emerges
from the shrubs
as if readying herself to march
again.
        Today the
peacefulness of the scene
belies the Rising, the digging of trenches
to slow the British, the demand
of women to buy a revolver and
trim their skirts for action.
                      She
survived because she was a woman,
a crazed touch of British chivalry,
a refusal to add her name to the
official Easter martyrs.
                  A commander,
she demanded equal treatment, but,
while the fourteen died
at Killmainham, she could
only protest.
             Today in the sun I saw
a woman feed the water birds
with the pond ringed by children.
If Constance Markiewicz had her way,
she would have died for this woman's freedom.

St. Stephens Green
1973

Lift Your Pint

Lift your pint
before the world dies
And the tide comes tumble
the crush and spill
of all of us
and the discovery

Lift your pint
touch wood
there's none above
to stop us
now we need the cheer
and soft insistence
old voices
keeping time
away from here

Sunday in Athlone

Just a country pub,
with a pile outside–a church
like a Mormon tomb.
                        No parking
for the outdoor sale of suits,
black suits, white shirts, open racks,
children all about.
                    Inside, children dance
in the slop.
          Pints all around, church is out.
Old fathers stagger while children hold them up.
Now and again the kids come poking
Through doors with narrow eyes---Da's not here,
on to the next pub.
                    And the girls
come in with their mass clothes on.
                            Da's not here,
on to the next pub.

A jump ahead of them all,
Da steps through the back, all of 18 stone,
"Set up a pint of plain," and the look
around
settles all
on a Sunday afternoon
in sunny Athlone.

Wolfe Tone Fractured

Over a smoking peat hob
Delaney, chiding the kids
upstairs, and warming his
ball of malt in his huge hands,
let forth with a powerful laugh
at the vandals who had just
poured their bomb on his
Wolfe Tone, blasting it
from St. Stephens Green
to the Bank of Ireland
and beyond.
               They'll get
another, he declared,
happy to cast a replacement
and lure the loyalists
out of hiding.
               They'll
just be making me rich,
and won't that be a shame,
he cried, amused at the
persistence of politics
in the isle.
               Wolfe Tone,
stirring Irish hearts a century
and a half ago, demanded
a revolution, recruited the French,
and was betrayed by spies. The
usual Irish playbook. But Tone,
a protestant patriot, and a man

whose sense of self elevated him
above the ordinary, refused the gibbet
and razored himself to glory.

Seamus Took My Hand

Seamus took my hand
to get away from the din,
sequestered in a nearby dorm
set aside for quality.
                      He was tired
of accolades and admiration,
now for a chance to open the Jamesons
and talk about the wildness
of Ireland past.
                  We had friends
in low places,
           like the bar
at the Beresford's where I met
Benedict Kiely, master of the
short story, master of the tall tale
and master of the sweet response to life
in the city.
            Seamus was your man
for gossip, talking about
Yeats, whose star was waning
in his eyes.
              Late in the evening
sipping with him, tastes of peat
and Irish soul blooming
as we laughed and poked fun at the moon,
talking of all things metrical
and illuminating, soft and telling,
the world of troubles sulking

around us, but we leaving it behind,
talking of all things musical
and all things meaningful,
and all things we knew we loved
alike.
     I took Yeats's side and said
how much he meant to me,
and how much Seamus's bog people meant to me,
but held back on telling him
how much it meant to be here with him.

Time Out

More than *Time Out*'s,
it is Joyce's Dublin
I find when I call to
mind moments of
meaningfulness.

The time I stood
on Howth head
thinking of Poldy
and Molly lying
on the gorse where
I would not lie
myself. But they
were there in my
mind, urging me
to look out upon
the water, fresh,
all of it a symbol
of love and lust,
urging me to
participate with
passion and time.

In the Ormond
Hotel, I sat with a
glass of Guinness
thinking of the
sirens who once

enlivened an hour
of the day. Two
Japanese tourists
snapped my photo
as if I were a bit
of the local color
and took me back
to Kyoto.
Then the ritual
return to Sandycove
and the Martello
Tower, not yet a
museum, looking in
the dark circular
room where Joyce
himself once slept.
I could barely see
the Pigeon House,
or the strand for
the crowd. A student
ragged me, asking if
it was the number 4 bus
that took me there. No,
it was chapter 1, page 1
that took me there.

Before I left, the critic,
Leslie Fiedler, pulled
me nearby, to take a
picture of him, a slight,
short, stubby man,
next to the iconic sign:
Forty Foot Men,

a dream he held dear,
and he posed as if the
moment enlarged him
to Brobingnagian stature.
Every day a satire.

Meeting Mary Lavin

She met me dressed in a
stunning tweed suit,
sitting in a pub with sherry
at hand.
      I ordered a small
lunch–she was abstemious–and
I unraveled the story from her.

An unpleasant memory of Storrs,
when her host of years ago
insisted she stay with his
family, made her put me off.
She never dreamed he was
a teetotaler, and one night
when an Irish friend took her
to dinner, she returned
in the dark with her Jameson,
only to drop it on the kitchen tiles
fumbling for a grip on the cork.

A sad disappointment, a gloomy
visit, with no pleasant memories
to make her glad to see me here,
inviting her to return.

Sheila the Maid in the Kitchen

So Chet tells her the one about the Irishman
back from Heaven talking about God: "Well, first off,
she's black."
                    Sheila might have been a wall.
Kitty waited for the punch-line and we just stared
in surprise at their dumbness.
                            "God's a Man," says Sheila
"Oh yes," Kitty says.
                    "And he's white.
Everyone knows that in Ireland."

                                  Wearing spats,
He'd be. Church of Ireland in Fitzwilliam Square
with a hundred thousand a year and a Rolls
with a black chauffeur.
                    Easy to see
in Herbert Park
          Just where the quality
must be.

All Too Irish

Richard slid us into Athlone
with a mission.
                    It was not a whisky wash,
or, not precisely so. It was a site
specific event.
                    We paid homage to the blue
door of Robert Burns, where a young Joyce
stumbled and peed establishing
his claim hidden in the Wake.
                          Richard the poet
blessed Burns's door himself,
in what he called an Irish moment.
                              It was high noon
in search of a perfect pint in a pub
that never washed its plumbing.
                          I thought of
Maeve, Aillil's great queen, who marked her turf
in the spring snow, astounding all
by the depth of her pee,
a warning to those who might affront her.

And what is a good pee, but a way of marking
where one is, the space one commands
if only for a nonce.
                  I myself, by the church
beside Yeats's grave, behind a distant buttress,
the bus raring to go, left my own mark
in an Irish way, intending it not
as a challenge, but an accolade.

In the Shebeen

Sunday after mass
in the far west of Ireland
with the basalt mountains of stone
edging into the Atlantic,
I sat quietly nursing my glass.
                        I was there
with neighborly folk politely
ignoring me while they told tales
in Irish.   The sounds were music
mixed with laughter.   The ceiling was
low, the light coming through small
windows, bright with a cloudless sky
seeming to me like the tales of Irish lore,
when armies roamed among the hills
and Cuchulain ruled the plain.   A romantic,
I felt drenched in Connemara, holding a dram
of poitin and anxious to know the gossip.
A darkhaired woman beside me said a word
I understood.   We spoke of nothing, and she asked
if I was a Dubliner.   When I said no, American,
she was surprised. "I thought by your accent," she said,
and I thought, My God, how far away we are in the West,
our words beguile us.

In the Muniment Room

In Trinity College, College Green
and Pearse Street, near Botany Bay,
much smaller than I expected,
like the headquarters of antiquity,
our table graced by scholarship,
a woman searching for news
of an eighteenth century nun,
a man across from me
whose metrical facial tic
tallied silently the minutes.

Imagining myself a normal reader,
I searched an edition of Milton
beached by lack of subscribers,
now unique and abandoned.
Its destiny, this tomb and my eyes.

My search was for a manuscript
in the hand of Walter Raleigh,
the Skeptic and soul of the School of Night.
His lines strong and rich in stoveblack ink,
glowed now as they once flamed abroad.

Exhausted and unsettled I took
the rooms on College Green,
fit, pale yellow, the scholar's cell
that once held Oscar Wilde.

I read until dark, when,

wrapt in Trinity's embracing
blanket, I fell asleep dreaming
of a literary life, alone on my bench
lips trembling, unbelieving all but
what is beautiful and what is rare.

Antrim

The startling beauty of Torr Head
sweetened the brickred sourness of Armagh
and Derry. We embraced the great rocks
and Irish grasses dipping into the sea
and rescued the memory
of Concubar and ancient Ireland.

Alluding to wars and Norse raids,
Torr's range of magnificent hills,
like a slumbering giant, curled
around the bay in Antrim.

Far out on the Head, a house facing westward,
stony, broken, windowless, unnatural,
stood an affront. Its insulting rectangles and ruin,
stricken chairs and mattresses in ugly
rooms and filthy floors made us rebel.
                                              Aghast,
we mounted the roof and stood
like victors surveying across
the few miles to Scotland, another
land that once raged against disorder
and ancient rapine.
                    Times change,
we change, and standing there gathering
our breath, we gave thanks for Torr's beauty,
which for us was a form of salvation.

Patrick Kavanagh

I made a point of sitting on his bench
on the Grand Canal at Mespil Road.

Thinking of him, a farmer walking
all the way to Dublin and knocking

on doors that turned him away, I
imagined the pain, but also the rage

that made him a legend on the bus
after hours, sparring with lesser poets,

roaring above the joyboys and girls
whose night out electrified Raglan Road.

The Great Hunger made him famous,
marking the pain my own people

suffered long years gone. He was
a dabbler in verse whose recognition

was wanted and got. He rejected his
most poetic work, choosing his rugged

unrefined lines, those filled with power
and harrowed directness, in a voice whose

strength came from lifting hundred pound
potato sacks onto carts on Iniskeen mornings.

His survival from the fall into the canal
and his lost lung in the hospital softened

him, gave him a new beginning, a moment
of renewal, and a claim on his inheritance.

As he said, his purpose in life was to have
no purpose as he sat idly by the waters.

I looked for his ghost on the Pembroke
Road and sniffed for his personality

because he asked us to remember him
disheveled, eccentric, his shoes untied.

Lucia Joyce

An Irish melange, all of literature
against all of literature.
                        Stephen,
grandson of Joyce, sat regally before us
in Venice, declaring the destruction of his
aunt's entire correspondence and life notes.
Lucia, in institutions for her adult years,
frustrated in her talents, befriended
by those who loved her father, was now
to be erased from literature.
                        But Michael Yeats
rose to protest. He saved his father's work,
gave it to the future. "Do the same," he said,
himself regal in manner, his sister by his side,
petitioning for Lucia's place in one more
Irish story. Let it be told.
                        When he sat down
Mary De Rachewiltz stood, declaring,
"I am Ezra Pound's daughter!" astounding
us all, as she pleaded with Stephen.
Demanding him not to do as men have often done,
remove a woman from history.
                        She stood
for literature, challenging a man who championed
his privacy, who condemned the very professors
James Joyce expected to read his work forever.

Seán O'Casey

When I was young in college
David Krause took a call
from him in our drama class.

O'Casey was a friend, a man
whose time was now, when
Juno was battling with the Paycock.

His work in Ireland stunned
the masses. Rising from
the slums of Dublin he

took the side of the middling
class, finding fun in the ambition
of the bourgeoisie.

Yes, he was a socialist,
a union man, a bystander
in the Easter rising, but

a critic of civil war, himself
not a shadow of a gunman,
but keen to cast his light

on the pain of Ireland's
hard men, who, posing as
righteous, bloodied the streets.

Even aristocratic Yeats saw
his talent and hurrahed his
skills in the Abbey. "You have

disgraced yourselves again," he told
the audience who rejected O'Casey's
 play whose title was the Irish flag.

But even Yeats, next year
turned his back on O'Casey's
condemnation of Empire

leaving him to harden his view
and set his stage abroad, where
Dublin spite was only a memory.

Coole Park

Still beautiful, when I was there
the initials in the copper beech
were vague, like memory eroded

Synge, the beautiful boy signed
here, with his mentor Yeats and
haughty Shaw and low O'Casey

even the future president Hyde
appears, but I could not find
Isabella Augusta, queen of Gort

whose genius knitted the future
together in a proud embrace of
ideals for Ireland, but not all who

saw the signs of a renaissance
agreed. Some who much later
harbored grievance burned her

stately home to the ground. Her
ideals remained to astound us all
wondering that ascendancy could

win in the end. Even virginal Yeats
succumbed to her widowed yearning
placing his name there along with his

wandering heart, searching for the wild swanns at Coole and finding kinship, understanding, courage, and grief.

Tain Bo Cuailgne

This ancient epic tells the tale
that echoes through our times

with Ailill and Maeve set against
Cuchulain, whose nemesis the

witchy Morigu, the shape changer,
threatens all. Ulster here and

Connacht and Munster there,
what still amazes me is the war

that shaped the world of Ferdía
Deirdre, Emer, Finnabair, Laeg,

and the spirits of the sidhe
was based on power, possession

and pride. The bull, the symbol
of stubborn force ruled all then

now later, the Tain tells us a tale
of carnage all too like our own.

James Joyce

Sunny Jim, to whom I have
given much of my life, as he

wished when he explained his
enigmas and puzzles were the

key to his immortality. But for me
they were neither puzzles or problems,

they were penetrations of the veil
Yeats called the Maya, insights that

sometimes left me tearful, feeling for
Bloom saying, "me and me now,"

when I knew his pain, how he felt,
how I would one day feel as he.

Joyce's many friends recognized
his genius, sometimes helped him

to bed in the dark, staggering, but
happy in his drink. There was that

time in the Aula Maxima when I
asked Maria Jolas if she was not

put out in having to haul him up

the stairs to bed and she raged

at me before a loyal crowd shocked
by her voice and the power of her

alarm, that I should even consider
it an inconvenience to help a genius

whose worth and friendship made
all things possible, that I should

think a friend such as she, the one
who befriended his Lucia after

he died, would even hesitate to help
him in whatever state she found him.

It was love, I could see. I failed her
test. My affection was insufficient.

Milton Keynes UK
Ingram Content Group UK Ltd.
UKHW012314040624
443649UK00007B/632